Deliverance Ministry Made Simple

Your Guide to Freedom

Patrice Gaillard, PhD, LCPC

Published in West Palm Beach, Florida by Cassy's Touch Publishing, LLC. Cassy's Touch Publishing, LLC books, journals, etc., may be ordered through booksellers worldwide or by contacting: www.cassystouch.com

The publisher is not responsible for websites (or their content) that are not owned by the publisher.

Scripture quotations marked KJV are taken from the King James Version. Public domain.

Scripture quotations marked MSG are taken from *The Message*, copyright © 1993, 2002, 2018 by Eugene H. Peterson. Used by permission of NavPress. All rights reserved. Represented by Tyndale House Publishers.

Scripture quotations marked (NIV) are taken from the Holy Bible, New International Version®, NIV®. Copyright © 1973, 1978, 1984, 2011 by Biblica, Inc.™ Used by permission of Zondervan. All rights reserved worldwide. www.zondervan.com The "NIV" and "New International Version" are trademarks registered in the United States Patent and Trademark Office by Biblica, Inc.™

Scripture quotations marked TPT are from The Passion Translation®. Copyright © 2017, 2018, 2020 by Passion & Fire Ministries, Inc. Used by permission. All rights reserved. ThePassionTranslation.com.

Visit the author's website at respiteforchange.com.

ISBN: 979-8-9892358-2-7 (softcover)
Library of Congress Control Number 2025903794

Printed in the United States of America

How To Use This Manual

1. For self-enrichment, self-edification and for self-deliverance
2. For training of church ministry teams to conduct deliverance
3. For training of para ministries to conduct deliverance
4. For use by church leadership to increase awareness in their congregation about deliverance ministry.

CONTENTS   PAGE

Preface

Deliverance ministry is often misunderstood, misrepresented, or narrowly defined by sensationalism rather than the foundational truth of Scripture. This manual was created to offer a clear, concise, and biblically sound understanding of deliverance—one that is centered on the finished work of Jesus Christ.

When many hear the term deliverance ministry, their minds immediately turn to dramatic encounters with demonic forces. While spiritual warfare is indeed real, the heart of deliverance is not about fear or spectacle—it is about freedom. It is about wholeness in Christ. Acts 10:38 declares, "God anointed Jesus of Nazareth with the Holy Spirit and power, and He went around doing good and healing all who were under the power of the devil, because God was with Him." This same Jesus is still healing, delivering, and restoring today through His Church. He has called His people to be vessels of His power, walking in authority, and bringing liberty to the oppressed.

This manual serves as a practical and spiritual guide to equip believers with the tools necessary for ministering deliverance and inner healing. It includes:
✓ A step-by-step approach to conducting deliverance sessions
✓ Sample prayers and forms for ministry settings
✓ Guidelines for self-deliverance and ministering in group settings

Drawing from years of experience in deliverance ministry, counseling, and training, I have seen firsthand the transformational power of God's healing hand. Through workshops, conferences, and intercessory gatherings across the U.S., Canada, and the Caribbean, I have worked with countless individuals seeking freedom from spiritual bondage and emotional wounds. My goal in writing this manual is to make deliverance practical, accessible, and biblically grounded so that the body of Christ may walk in its full inheritance of healing and wholeness.

My prayer is that as you journey through this manual, you will not only receive revelation but also be empowered to bring the healing power of Christ to those in need.

May this resource be a tool for breakthrough, transformation, and lasting freedom in Christ.

Patrice Gaillard, PhD, LCPC
Christian Counselor, Deliverance Minister, Author

May God himself, the God who makes everything holy and whole, make you holy and whole, put you together—spirit, soul, and body—and keep you fit for the coming of our Master, Jesus Christ.

1 Thessalonians 5:23 The Message

Introduction

This material has been developed by Respite for Change Counseling services, inner healing, and deliverance ministry to add to the many other resources currently on the market about the ministry of deliverance and inner healing. I hope to offer even more insight on the practical aspect of this ministry with an emphasis to bring clarity to some of the misconceptions about deliverance.

Much of the insight I will offer in this material, I gained from personal experience in administering deliverance, from encounters with church leaders and from trainings I have received from Invicta University, Righteous Act Ministries under the International Society for Deliverance Ministers, and from the Centers for Christian Counseling. This is in addition to the very many written and online trainings by Derek Prince and others.

Although there may be different styles of administration and delivery of deliverance offered by different organizations and ministers, the one fact that remains true and will never change is that Jesus is the one who introduced the ministry of deliverance in the bible. As followers of Jesus Christ, we do what Jesus did and that is to preach the gospel message, heal the sick, heal the broken hearted (inner healing), and drive out demons. I am thankful to Pastor Mark Chase, the founder of Invicta Ministries and Invicta University for his teaching, training, mentorship, and encouragement and for remaining steadfast to continue the practice of this ministry of deliverance, and I continue to glean from his expertise.

There has been increasing emphasis placed on the ministry of deliverance over the past few years and many people have acknowledged the need for deliverance and have taken the initiative to submit to the deliverance process to be set free from mental torment, addictions, diseases, and all sorts of perversions. When we look at those who are stepping forward to acknowledge the need for deliverance, we find that those in leadership can be very reluctant to embark on this spiritual journey of deliverance due to concerns of being mishandled, lack of discretion and most importantly due to all the controversy surrounding the ministry of deliverance. Their concerns are valid. As one who conducts deliverance ministry, I am confronted and challenged many times with doubts about the whole idea of deliverance, and with questions about if deliverance is for born-again believers. I have also been challenged many times about the methods applied for both deliverance and inner healing. The controversies, disbelief, and criticism of deliverance ministry have caused many to turn away from administering deliverance as well as discouraged many from seeking deliverance for themselves. This group includes church and ministry leaders. This is a great disservice to the body of Christ. I believe deliverance is indicated and needed now more than ever in the body of Christ; leaders included. I also believe deliverance is an end-time ministry. The picture that has been projected of deliverance is very skewed, to say the least.

When people hear the word "deliverance," they automatically think of, something from a movie scene- demons yelling, rolling on the floor, and abusing their hosts. That is a very gruesome picture, and I would not ever want to submit myself to such a process. In fact, I have been through the process of deliverance, and it was a very positive experience for me. None of what I mentioned above happened. I was handled with care and compassion; I received deliverance counseling as well and was educated on how to remain free. I did receive freedom and healing at my deliverance encounters. It is for this reason that I advocate for deliverance ministry. I believe deliverance is the children's bread. Matthew 15:22-26 tells of an encounter between Jesus and a Canaanite woman with a demon-possessed daughter. Jesus made the statement in verse 26 to show that he was sent to bring deliverance to the lost sheep of Israel. He referred to deliverance in that passage as "the children's bread."

It is not right to take the children's bread and toss it to the dogs. Matthew 15:26 NIV

I also believe deliverance places the believer in a position to live the abundant life Jesus died for his followers to have. Why should we, as followers of Christ, remain bound by such as anxiety, fear, torment, addictions, perversions, poverty, and the like when we are the beneficiaries of the finished work of the cross? It is clearly written in the bible that we have been given every spiritual blessing in the heavenly realms and by His divine power Jesus has given us all things pertaining to life and Godliness.

Praise be to the God and Father of Our Lord Jesus Christ, who has blessed us in the heavenly realms with every spiritual blessing in Christ. Ephesians 1:3 NIV

His divine power has granted *to us* all things *that* pertain *to* life *and* godliness, *through the knowledge of him who called us to his own glory and excellence. 2 Peter 1:3 NIV.*

So, how should we look at the ministry of deliverance? What is the correct perspective? What is the ministry of deliverance? Is deliverance for born-again believers? What does it really look like, and what can I expect from a deliverance encounter? With guidance from the Holy Spirit, we will provide answers to those questions; however, I believe the Holy Spirit is the best person to answer those questions. It is my prayer that everyone reading this material will seek deeper understanding and personal revelation about the ministry of deliverance from the Holy Spirit.

And that you will not only seek deliverance for yourself and become an advocate for deliverance ministry, but that you will become a practitioner of deliverance to allow the Holy Spirit to use you to set others free.

1

What is the Ministry of Deliverance?

I prefer to use the term "ministry of deliverance" because, it is a very practical aspect of service to the children of God. The Hebrew word for ministry is *sharat*, which means to be in service to another person. So, when I administer deliverance, I am providing a service to the person sitting in front of me.

Webster dictionary defines the word deliverance to mean liberation, salvation, rescue, and freedom. The dictionary also compares the word deliverance to the process of a jury delivering a verdict in the court room.

From the biblical perspective, the Apostle Paul writes in Galatians 1:3-4: *Grace to you and peace from God the Father and Our Lord Jesus Christ, who gave himself for Our sins to **rescue** us from this present evil age, according to the will of our God and Father.* Gal. 1:3-4NIV

The Greek word for *rescue* in Galatians 1:4 denotes not rescue *out of* the world but rather **rescue *from* the power of evil**. In other words, we see one aspect of deliverance here in that Jesus gave himself so that those who would accept him as Lord and Savior would be "***rescued***" or "***delivered***" from the power of evil. I also want to point out that the word Paul uses for 'evil' in Galatians 1:4 is *poneros,* which comes from the word 'pernicious. Satan is synonymous with the word 'evil' or *poneros*. Satan's agenda is to pollute and corrupt the systems of God's world. Pernicious evil therefore seeks to corrupt and enslave people in cycles of dysfunction, sin, and death. By the power of the gospel, followers of Jesus are delivered or rescued from *the power* of this corruption to live and serve the cause of Christ to bring healing and deliverance to those bound under Satan's power. The passage in Luke reads- *He has sent me to heal the brokenhearted, to preach deliverance to the captives. Luke 4:18* NIV

The King James Bible dictionary defines 'deliverance' as "release from captivity, slavery, oppression, or any restraint," and also defines deliverance "as to rescue from danger."

The word 'deliverance' is used in nine of the sixteen chapters in the book of Mark in the bible and the word 'deliver' is used 296 times in the bible.

One of the most common beliefs I hear in the argument against deliverance ministry is that the finished work of the cross took care of everything, and no further deliverance is needed. And yet the same individuals continue to struggle with depression, sin, anxiety, and cycles of dysfunction. The finished work of the cross has granted us the **ultimate deliverance** which is salvation or rescue from the kingdom of darkness to the kingdom of God, from the power of sin and from eternal damnation, which is the consequence of sin. Without the salvation found in Jesus Christ alone by accepting Him as Lord and Savior, humanity is enslaved by sin according to Romans 6: 20-22 NIV. Jesus became sin that humanity would be given a choice of freedom from slaves to a life of sin and to be reconciled to God the Father in righteousness. This can only happen when we repent and believe. We must make the choice to repent, believe, and confess Christ as Lord.

For God so loved the world that he gave his one and only Son, that whoever believes in him shall not perish but have eternal life. John 3:16 NIV

If you declare with **your mouth**, "Jesus is Lord," and believe in your heart that God raised him from the dead, **you** will be saved. Romans 10:9 NIV

The argument is that when a person becomes born again, all things become new.

Therefore, if any man be in Christ, he is a new creature: old things are passed away; behold, all things are become new. 2 Corinthians 5:17 NIV.

In as much as this is true, it is also true that "man" was created as a tripartite being in the image and in the likeness of God who is Father, Son, and Spirit. Man was also created spirit, soul, and body (tripartite). The true nature of man is spirit. Man has a soul, which consists of the mind, will, and emotions. So, when a person is born again, he is given a new spirit, or his spirit is regenerated, or born again and now that person has a new nature. This process is a one-time event. However, the process of transformation of the soul must occur.

God created man in his own image, in the image of God he created them; male and female he created them. Genesis 1:27 NIV.

The soul and the body are not automatically made new when we become born again. Often it is a process and the beginning of the journey. We must allow the Holy Spirit to transform us from the old carnal person we were into the new spirit person Christ has made us to be. The old person that was led by the soul will still include the works of the flesh and demonic influences we either inherited due to covenants established by our ancestors or the consequences of our personal sins. The Apostle Paul writes in the book of Ephesians:

And you also were included in Christ when you heard the message of truth, the gospel of your salvation. When you believed, you were marked in him with a seal, the promised Holy Spirit, who is a deposit guaranteeing our inheritance until the redemption of those who are God's possession to the praise of his glory. Ephesians 1:13-14 NIV.

The believer of Jesus Christ is marked and becomes God's possession upon accepting Christ earnestly as Lord and is guaranteed a divine and ultimate inheritance. The Holy Spirit now continues to do the work of saving, rescuing, and delivering those who are his. He makes his power, grace, and help available as he works out his salvation and deliverance in us.

...continue to work out your salvation with fear and trembling, for it is God who works in you to will and to act in order to fulfill his good pleasure. Philippians 2: 12b-13 NIV

As we see in the scripture above, there is a working out to be done after we confess Christ and say the salvation prayer. Yes, we have a new spirit, but the soul and body must catch up to the new person we have become in Christ. It is not by our strength this "work out your salvation" can be done, it is Christ who does the working out by the power of the Holy Spirit. As an example, if a person had diabetes pre-salvation, chances are they will still have diabetes after their salvation encounter. If a person had mental illness or anxiety before the salvation encounter, they will probably still have the illness after the salvation encounter. If a person was addicted to alcohol or drugs, they may still struggle with the addiction after praying the salvation prayer. There is a "working out" that needs to be done to set boundaries to keep the person from falling into the temptation of the addiction. Deliverance ministry makes it possible to address the areas of dysfunction, addiction, and sickness to go to the root system to uproot out those evil seeds, which is only possible because of the finished work of the cross. The Bible teaches us that everything that was not designed by God for the believer must be uprooted. Therefore, the salvation encounter does not necessarily eliminate the addictions and dysfunctions but makes it possible for believers to receive freedom in their soul and body by the ministry of deliverance accompanied by consistent Biblical counseling and discipleship. Demonic or evil oppressions are addressed by deliverance; however, mental strongholds must be pulled down.

Every plant that my Father in heaven has not planted Himself will be pulled up by the roots. Matthew 15:13-14 NIV

False beliefs and habits that were developed over many years must be addressed by Biblical counseling, discipleship, and the mind must be renewed according to Romans 12:1-2.

Do not be conform to the pattern of this world, but be transformed by the renewing of your mind. Romans 12:2 NIV

Satan will continue to harass believers until he is confronted and driven out by the power of God. **The process of deliverance** is to enforce the finished work of the cross, to superimpose our salvation and new identity in Christ; as well as to confront the evil works of Satan by his demons in the lives of believers and drive them out.

John 10:10 shows us that Jesus came to give the believer the abundant life.

The thief does not come except to steal, and to kill, and to destroy. I have come that they may have life, and that they may have it more abundantly. John 10:10 NIV

But if I with the finger of God cast out Devils, no doubt the kingdom of God has come upon you. Luke 11:20 NIV

God's desire is for his people to come to wholeness while on this earth; it is God's will for his people to be healed and completely whole in mind, body, and spirit. **Deliverance** is a ministry of restoration and healing birthed out of God's love and compassion for His people. It is a part of the package of our salvation; it is a resource God has given his people to deal with the evil works of Satan in their lives. Deliverance is concerned with the overall wellness of God's people. To put it plainly, when Jesus encountered a person with a demon, he drove the demon out. We do what Jesus did, so when we encounter a person with a demon, we drive the demon out within the proper boundaries. That is the Ministry of Deliverance.

Going back to the story with the Canaanite woman who went to Jesus seeking deliverance for her daughter who was demon-possessed in Matt. 15:22-28. What did Jesus mean by "the children's bread in reference to deliverance? Bread is representation of provision—it is food. Bread for the children of Israel was a representation of God's power and love because when the children of Israel grumbled against Moses because of hunger, God met their need by sending them manna, the bread of heaven. So, deliverance is the actual power of God in action in the lives of his people working out their salvation or rescue. God himself is the deliverer, and he has authorized his followers to continue this ministry of deliverance in the aspect of driving out evil or Satan's demons from the lives of God's people so they can live the abundant life of Christ. Jesus gave this charge to his disciples, and this is the same charge to us today.

As you go, proclaim this message: 'The kingdom of heaven has come near.' Heal the sick, raise the dead, cleanse those who have leprosy, drive out demons. Freely you have received; freely give. Matthew 10: 7-8 NIV

2

What Does Deliverance Look Like?

James 4:7 TPT reads: "...*surrender to God. Stand up to the devil and resist him, and he will flee in agony.*" So, deliverance from the influence of demons can only be possible by a life of submission and surrender to the Lord Jesus Christ. The foundation for deliverance is submission to God. I would go as far to say that one aspect of resisting the devil as we are commanded to in James 4:7 is to submit to the process called technical deliverance, where the believer sits through an encounter with a servant of God trained to administer deliverance. The process of technical deliverance is very much like a courtroom setting; **God** is the righteous Judge. God is the one who brings the deliverance. The deliverance minister is the **Defense Attorney** ordained and deputized by the Holy Spirit as the vessel to defend the person receiving deliverance from evil oppressions or demons from **Satan**, the accuser of the brethren. The deliverance minister prepares the case and now places the demons on the witness stand. Demons are placed under oath before **Jehovah God**. The deliverance minister is then guided by the Holy Spirit to lead the person receiving ministry through a process of repentance, forgiveness, renouncing, closing spiritual doors and revoking all access given to the enemy to drive out the evil spirits by the power of Jesus Christ. I would also like to point out that the deliverance encounter involves much more than casting out demons, in fact that is the last phase of the encounter. The deliverance encounter usually takes about two to three hours, most of the time is spent preaching the gospel message and evaluating the person's understanding of what it means to be a follower of Jesus. Secondly, time is taken for Biblical counseling to help the person understand the need for submission to God and the need for forgiveness. The deliverance minister also takes time to educate on the differences between mental strongholds and works of the flesh that are not demonic and therefore cannot be cast out; but requires discipleship. The ministry of deliverance ideally is not a standalone process but works hand in hand with inner healing and discipleship in the word of God. The ministry of deliverance is a process and not an intervention. We can compare the process of deliverance to the children of Israel apprehending their promise land a little at time.

The LORD your God will drive out those nations before you, little by little. You will not be allowed to eliminate them all at once, or the wild animals will multiply around you. But the LORD your God will deliver them over to you, throwing them into great confusion until they are destroyed. Deuteronomy. 7:22-23 NIV

The LORD your God will drive out these nations before **you** *little by little.* **You will not** *be enabled to* **eliminate them all** *at* **once.** *Exodus 23:29 NIV*

The person receiving deliverance must be an active participant in the process. Deliverance must be supported by ongoing discipleship, as we previously mentioned. As the person goes through the process of deliverance, they also need to be discipled in the word of God to live a life full of the Spirit and fully submitted to the Lordship of Jesus Christ. The Bible teaches us that after an evil spirit comes out of a person, the demons become homeless and will try to return with seven more demons to the human body where they once lived if they find the person empty, the final state of the person will be worse than before. For this reason, people are to be properly counseled and educated on the concept of deliverance. Administering deliverance should not consider the skill or the anointing of the deliverance minister or the vessel the Holy Spirit is using. Although those factors are important, the priority is about the sustainable freedom of the person getting deliverance. Anyone serving in deliverance ministry must be prepared to provide biblical counsel and discipleship to empower those receiving deliverance to sustain their freedom. The idea is not to create a cycle of dependence on deliverance or the minister. People must be taught to depend on the Lord and not on a process of deliverance. To not educate in demonic re-entry can be seen as an ethical issue as well.

When an impure spirit comes out of a person, it goes through arid places seeking rest and does not find it. Then it says, 'I will return to the house I left.' When it arrives, it finds the house unoccupied, swept clean, and put in order. Then it goes and takes with it seven other spirits more wicked than itself, and they go in and live there. And the final condition of that person is worse than the first. Matthew 12:43-45 NIV

We also see in John 5:14 after Jesus had healed the man on the Sabbath day, he later found him in the temple and said to him *"see, you are well again. Stop sinning or something worse may happen to you." John 5:14 NIV.*

When clients call our ministry for deliverance, we recommend a minimum of two counseling sessions before the deliverance encounter is scheduled to help the person understand their identity in Christ, what deliverance is, and how the demons entered their life. And two or more counseling sessions are scheduled after the deliverance encounter to help the person understand how to remain free. We recommend they continue discipleship with their church for continued growth and maturity in Christ. In my personal experience, I found that very few people are willing to commit to this process.

3

Is Deliverance Biblical?

The question of whether deliverance is biblical I believe can be answered in the fact that the word deliverance is defined by the dictionary as salvation and rescue. To receive God's salvation is to receive God's deliverance and rescue. As previously mentioned, the word 'deliverance' is used in nine of the sixteen chapters in the book of Mark in the bible and the word 'deliver' is used 296 times in the bible. Jesus came to offer deliverance or salvation and rescue from the kingdom of darkness to the kingdom of God.

Jesus introduced the driving out of demons from people, including those in the place of worship which implies believers. **Nine of the sixteen chapters** in the book of Mark mentions deliverance from demons. The practice of driving out demons or deliverance from demons is documented in the bible.

Jesus sent out the disciples with the following instructions: "Do not go among the Gentiles or enter any town of the Samaritans. Go rather to the lost sheep of Israel. As you go, proclaim this message: 'The kingdom of heaven has come near. Heal the sick, raise the dead, cleanse those who have leprosy,] drive out demons. Freely you have received; freely give. Matthew 10:5-8 NIV

The reason the Son of God was made manifest (visible) was to undo (destroy, loosen, and dissolve) the works the devil [has done]. 1 John 3:8b NIV

It is very clear from the scriptures above that Jesus himself cast out demons. 1 John 3:8b shows us that Jesus came to destroy every work of the devil, and He deputized his followers to join in with Him in setting the captives free. That is the directive from Jesus to every believer, to drive out impure spirits.

4

Is Deliverance from the Perspective of Driving Out Demons for Believers?

To answer that question, we will look at the nature and operation of the demonic realm and the nature of man.

Demons are earthbound, disembodied unclean spirit beings.

The demons were cast out of heaven with Lucifer when he rebelled against God (Rev. 12:3-9). Lucifer, the devil, is the boss and the demons are his agents. The demonic kingdom is organized in order of hierarchy and rank. Demons operate in groups; they have minds, wills, emotions, and can communicate with one another. They recognize the presence of other demons in people, and they are very wicked. Demons' spirits are always seeking a host- a human body to indwell so they can find expression. Demon spirits can speak and project thoughts in the minds of people. They act and express emotions through their hosts. You will know a tree by its fruit, correct? Such as it is with demons. You can identify their existence by the fruit of the person under their influence. A lying demon will cause their hosts to lie; a death demon will cause death either by disease, sickness, accidents, suicide, murder and death to relationships, marriage, and ministries; a perversion demon will cause their hosts to be promiscuous and commit acts of perversion. Some demons are very subtle while others can be very aggressive. Demons also cause disabilities, addictions, stagnation, mental illness and all sorts of dysfunction and defilement to their hosts. Demons treat the human body they invade as their home. See what the Bible says: "When the unclean spirit is gone out of a man, he walketh through dry places, seeking rest, and finds none, then he saith, I **will return into my house** from whence I came out." *Matt.12:43-44 NIV* This verse in Matthew 12:43 shows us that evil spirits "came out"- that means they had to be in the person to come out. Secondly, verse 44 shows the evil spirits which are demons said, "I will return to my house." This shows us that the demons have intelligence, thought and will. They make decisions and they consider the human body their homes. Demons are never random in their activities; they come with a specific assignment from their boss, Satan, to bring **defilement, hinder, abuse, persecute**, **steal, kill, destroy, exploit** their hosts and to **quench God's spirit** in the believer. What has the thief come to steal, kill, and destroy? The believer's intimacy with God, marriages, families, relationships, health, finances, ministries, etc. A person may be sure of their salvation, and yet still struggle with demonic oppression that can be evidenced by vicious cycles of dysfunction. **Unclean spirits or demons should never ever, ever be tolerated** by the believer, especially one in leadership. As soon as unclean spirits are discovered they should be driven out- they are invaders and trespassers.

Unclean spirits that are not confronted and driven out simply remain. Unclean spirts cannot be ignored, prayed through, counseled, or reasoned with, they are to be **cast out in the name of Jesus!**

How is it possible for a demon to get access to a born-again child of God? God places a hedge of protection around every believer, but sin breaks this hedge and gives demons access or legal rights to harass or influence the life of the believer. A born-again believer **CANNOT** be **possessed** by evil spirits because they belong to God; but demons can certainly harass and torment the believer either from the inside; in their soul and body or from the outside. Understand that God allows the demons access to the believer because of unrepented sin- personal, generational, or sin across an ungodly soul tie and due to dissociation of the core person. It is unrepented sin that gives Satan access to the believer. I believe we have established how demons operate and how they can access the believer in the simplest form.

The answer to the question, "is the driving out of demons for the born-again believers?" is clear. We also see Jesus driving out demons from the people in the synagogue. Today's synagogue is the church.

Mark 1:39 reads: *Jesus traveled throughout Galilee, preaching in their synagogues, and driving out demons.*

I think it is safe to assume Jesus cast demons out from the believers in the church. Casting out demons in the church was a very common practice in Jesus's time and should be the same for us today. The church of Jesus Christ should be viewed as a hospital where the sick come to get healed, where those bound can come to be set free, where the demonized can come to be delivered in the name of Jesus. Biblical accounts of Jesus ministering deliverance are recorded in Mark 1:23-34, Luke 13, Matt. 8:16, Matt. 8:28-34 and many more. Jesus trained his disciples to minister deliverance, gave them authority and sent them out to do the ministry of deliverance to set the captives free. I admit, there is nothing glamourous about the process of driving demons out, but it is not as gruesome as it is made out to be. The picture Jesus painted for us is that the demons were commanded to come out and they obeyed Jesus. Well, when a believer who believes in deliverance issues the command to a demon to come out in the name of Jesus, the demons must obey just as they did in the day of Jesus. Demons can be commanded to come out quietly. Demons are never in control; Holy Spirit is the one in control.

I believe in the concept of "do what Jesus did." Jesus did drive out demons by the power of God in the church and from believers. 1 Thes. 5:23 teaches us a bit more about the concept of deliverance from the perspective of salvation. In the scripture below, Paul reinforces for us the reality of the "working out our salvation" which has the goal for the believer to be kept blameless in spirit, soul, and body. The believer is to be set apart for God and God himself will transform the believer into the likeness of Christ- that is the end goal. Without going into the full doctrine of sanctification as this is not the purpose of this material, it is sufficient to say the enemy of man's soul also has an end goal to ultimately destroy the believer. How the enemy works is through his demonic attacks in the lives of God's people. God's plan is sanctification, so the believer looks like him, Satan's plan is defilement, so the believer looks like him.

May God himself, the God of peace sanctify you through and through. May your whole spirit, soul and body be kept blameless at the coming of our Lord Jesus Christ. 1 Thes. 5:23 NIV

When we understand God's design for the believer is to be set apart and kept blameless soul, body, and spirit, and we also understand Satan's purpose is to defile and destroy the believer, we can safely say that deliverance is for believers as God has given us the means in which he can set us free from Satan's purposes. "Deliverance" is the children's bread. We are admonished in the word of God not to be ignorant to the devices of Satan, lest he takes advantage of us. (2 Cor. 2:11NIV) If we choose to remain ignorant to Satan's devices and remain inactive, know that what is not confronted in our lifetime and evicted remains to continue its course and transfers to the next generation. We see this in the tendency of alcoholism, drug addiction, adultery, and suicide to run in families. Let us not give Satan any advantage over us. Deliverance is for all believers, church leaders, and ministry leaders. Leaders are in a position of influence with the ability to have both a positive or negative impact in the lives of people, including children and others who are very vulnerable. Therefore, leaders need deliverance first and foremost so that they can lead from a place of wholeness. Leaders are certainly not exempt from the assaults of the enemy. It is crucial for those who have been wounded and traumatized to get healing and deliverance instead of covering up. Many believers, including leaders, carry past emotional wounds and childhood trauma that were never fully healed, even after salvation. Past emotional wounds are often referred to as a broken heart, soul wounds, and dissociation of the core. Unhealed soul wounds or dissociation of the core also serve as an open door for demons to access the believer. Therefore, inner healing is a crucial part of the deliverance encounter.

It is my prayer for the body of Christ to create more and more safe spaces for believers and leaders to get deliverance ministry. I also hope that this material will help to dispel the fears and misconceptions of deliverance ministry. The other argument presented is that demons cannot co-exist with the Holy Spirit in the born-again believer. It is possible for a person to have the Holy Spirit and still be under the demonic influence. We previously explained that man was created as a tripartite being, spirit, soul, and body. The image below depicts the 3 parts of man.

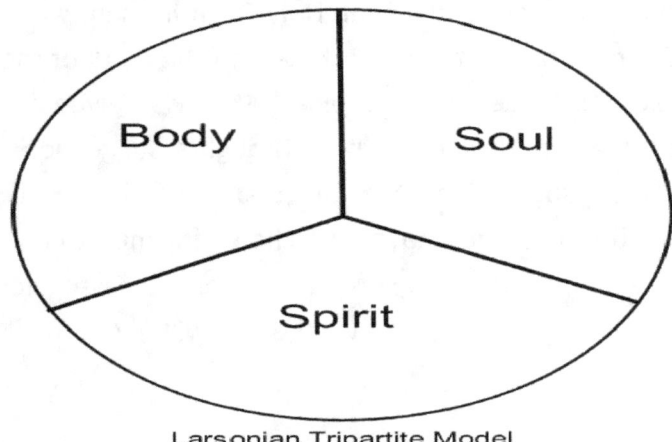

Larsonian Tripartite Model

The Spirit: The believer is given a new spirit at conversion that is sealed by the Holy Spirit of God. The new spirit we receive at conversion is made right with God, however, the believer does not also get a born-again body and soul. It is a process, and as we previously mentioned, the Holy Spirit will begin the work of transformation/sanctification in the believer. The goal is for the Holy Spirit to eventually rule over the soul and the body, and the believer will bear the fruit of the spirit according to Gal. 5:16-23 NIV. This requires the believer to choose.

The Soul: The soul of the believer is the will, mind, and emotions. The soul as previously mentioned, is not saved at salvation but is being transformed. Rom 12:2 tells us that the mind must be renewed after salvation. This is where the demons enter and attack the believer because of believing the lies of the devil, which can degenerate into mental strongholds. The other area of the soul where the enemy attacks is when dissociation of the core is present. This is a process where the mind fractures to encapsulate pain and emotional trauma. Dissociation of the core causes the person to be double-minded and unstable. Demons take advantage of this and uses the dissociation as a point of entry to the believer's life. Demonic attacks also come as a result of unrepented **sin** across the 3-pathways of sin- personal sin, sin done to those under authority or sin done across an ungodly soul tie. More detail is provided in the phases of deliverance.

The Body: is the shell that holds the spirit and the soul. Demons can inflict the human body with fiery darts, disease, infirmity, and disability.

The image below depicts how the presence of demon invasion in the soul brings interference and quenches the work of the Holy Spirit in man. You might ask, "if Holy Spirit is all powerful, how can demons interfere with the work of the Holy Spirit in the believer?" The answer is "freedom of choice." Man was given free will; man must choose. The demons work in the mind to inject thoughts, suggestions, and temptations. Holy spirit is also making suggestions; the still quiet voice of the Holy Spirit is always at work, drawing man to Himself but leaves the choice for man to make. Remember, as previously mentioned, it is sin that gives the demons access. Therefore, man must choose to submit to God and resist the devil; then he will flee.

Satan and his demons project thoughts and lies to the believer's minds. When the believer accepts the thoughts and lies, they come into agreement and partnership with

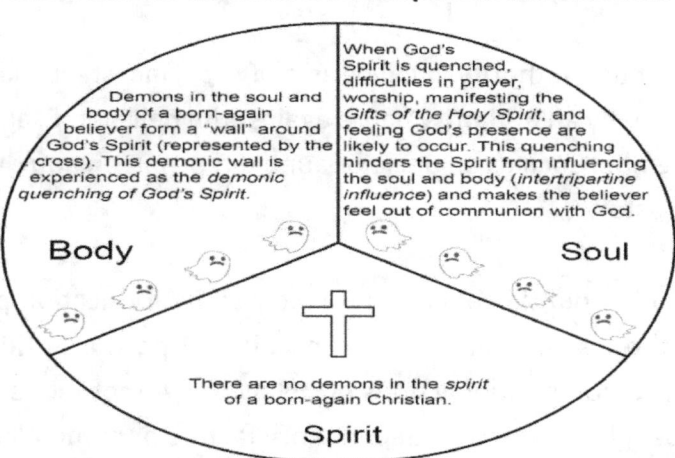

The Demons Quench God's Spirit in the Believer

Demons in the soul and body of a born-again believer form a "wall" around God's Spirit (represented by the cross). This demonic wall is experienced as the *demonic quenching of God's Spirit.*

When God's Spirit is quenched, difficulties in prayer, worship, manifesting the *Gifts of the Holy Spirit,* and feeling God's presence are likely to occur. This quenching hinders the Spirit from influencing the soul and body (*intertripartine influence*) and makes the believer feel out of communion with God.

Body

Soul

There are no demons in the *spirit* of a born-again Christian.

Spirit

"I am born again, but something isn't right."

the demons. Hence, by this agreement, access is granted. Ephes. 4:27 teaches we are not to give the devil a foothold. There are dangers in coming in agreement with the lies of Satan because thoughts create behaviors. What we believe will eventually influence how we behave. The lies we believe have the potential to degenerate into mental strongholds. Demon spirits will utilize strongholds of the mind to access the believer and bring torment. The mental strongholds and faulty beliefs must be pulled down according to 2 Cor. 10:4-5 and addressed by teaching the person how to apply truth found in God's word. This is done in the pre- and post-deliverance counseling phases.

Dissociation of the core is the result of childhood trauma or emotional wounds at any age. The soul fractures to create a part to hold trauma and pain so that the core person can continue to function. The soul can also fracture to create parts to help the core person perform tasks the core would not be able to perform. This is technically sin demons can hold on to because of the failure to depend on the Holy Spirit. It is God's will for His people to depend on Him and not hold on to pain or trauma. Dissociation of the core also represents a state of double-mindedness, which is a lack of faith.

Cast *all* **your** *anxiety on* **him** *because he* **cares** *for you. 1 Pet. 5:7 NIV*

A double-minded man is unstable in all his ways. James 1:8 NIV

Personal sin results from the choices the believer makes to disobey God's word and counsel.

Sin done to those under authority involves acts of rape, incest, abuse, manipulation, or any random violation by an authority figure against the believer. Examples are a parent, an older family member such as an uncle or aunt, a teacher, an adult to a child, an older sibling or even a pastor.

Sin across an ungodly soul tie could be represented by fornication partners- both the relationship and the act are sinful. Drug and alcohol partners- this is an unhealthy relationship that promotes sinful actions or behaviors. A mother can have an ungodly soul tie with her daughter due to co-dependency factors or manipulation.

Generational sins are those faulty foundations passed down the bloodline. Examples are all the women in the family control their husbands and that is expected and promoted from generation to generation. All the men in the family cheat on their wives, or evil covenants that are passed down- every child born in the family is dedicated to a particular god, or all the children born in the family are bathed in a ritual bath ceremony.

All the above practices leave an imprint in the believer's soul, and they must be renounced by choice and broken in the name of Jesus; then the demons attached can be driven out. Then inner healing is ministered to the person to address core dissociation and allow Holy Spirit to heal the soul wounds and trauma.

As a believer, if you experience any of the following symptoms, you could be under demonic oppression: Difficulty to worship, falling asleep during the preaching at church often, dysfunctional cycles that you cannot break (repeated toxic relationships, failed relationships, you love God, but feel constantly drawn to sin and after sinning you hate yourself and can't understand why you do the things you do) repeated bad dreams and nightmares, unexplained illnesses that doctors can't figure out, multiple illnesses, addictions you cannot break, anxiety, fear, panic attacks, depression and more.

God has a plan, a call, and a purpose for every born-again believer to carry out good works of the kingdom that God has prepared in advance. Demonic assault in the lives of the believer is always a snare and hinders the believer from living in God's call and purposes. It is therefore to the glory of God when a believer gets delivered and set free from demonic oppressions.

For we are God's handiwork, created in Christ Jesus to do good works, which God prepared in advance for us to do. Ephesians 2:10 NIV

God has made provisions for his people to get free so that he can use them to carry out his purposes. Believers cannot be effective in carrying out the plans and purposes of God if they remain bound and double minded. It's time to put the Ax to the root of everything that HINDERS, AFFLICTS and DEFILES. Jesus has made a way for those who belong to him to be disentangled from those things. He has given us the ministry of DELIVERANCE.

The ministry of deliverance is to be seen from the perspective of service to one another. It is my desire that we will see the need for deliverance, seize the opportunity, and serve in this capacity with gladness. God, who is the rewarder, will reward abundantly.

The sections that follow will provide a guide to prepare you to administer deliverance. It is recommended to work in teams of at least two. Women should minister to women and men should minister to men.

The answer to the question, "what I can expect from a deliverance encounter?" is answered in the following pages that include the phases of deliverance with a step-by-step guide. Also included are the forms you will need to set up a deliverance encounter; sample questionnaire, sample personal spiritual profile that can be used to prepare for the deliverance encounter, sample prayers and sample spirit root inventory. Lastly, it is strongly recommended that persons who desire to answer the call to administer deliverance must abide in Christ and submit their lives as a consecrated vessel onto God.

5

What is Inner Healing?

Inner healing is a work of the Holy Spirit. Psalms 147:3 in the AMPC clearly states Jesus heals the broken hearted and binds up their wounds, curing their pains and their sorrows.

We also see in Jeremiah 30:17 NIV where God was speaking about his people- *"I will restore you to health and heal your wounds declared the Lord, because you are called an outcast..."* This speaks of rejection; they were rejected and cast out of their land.

A classic example of inner healing is found in the story of the woman with the issue of blood in Luke 8:43-48 NIV In verse 48, Jesus said to the woman, *"Daughter, be of good comfort, thy faith hath made thee whole, go in peace."* In addition to healing the woman physically, Jesus ministered inner healing to the woman. He called the woman "daughter." The fact that he called her "daughter" spoke directly to the woman's soul. She was most likely dealing with rejection, poor self-esteem, isolation, deprivation, loneliness, and she was an outcast- not allowed to be in community because of her issue. Jesus calling her "daughter" was to communicate identity, a sense of belonging, in that you are now family, and you have found identity with the Master. He not only healed physically, but he healed her emotional wounds. This woman had been treated as an outcast and rejected for a long time.

We, as believers serving in the ministry of deliverance, are enforcers of God's word, we position ourselves in faith as facilitators for the Holy Spirit to work through us to administer inner healing.

Inner healing is essentially to heal and restore to wholeness the fragmented human soul which is comprised of the mind, the will, and the emotions. Inner healing, much like deliverance, in most cases is a process.

What is a soul wound? How are they inflicted?

For us to understand the root cause of soul wounds, we need to take a brief look at the basic stages of human development.

Psychiatrist Erik Erickson developed the stages of development in 1956, and based on the stages of development Erickson shows us that it is the formative years of a child's life that impacts their cognitive, social, emotional, and physical development beginning from ages 0-8 years old.

During those years, the brain and neurobiological development are the fastest after birth. What happens to a child in these formative years has been proven to have great impact on their physical development, mental development, and overall success in life.

Soul wounds can be a direct result of adverse childhood experiences in the formative years, originating from our parents and family of origin 90% of the time, which I believe are orchestrated by the enemy to keep us from fulfilling God's mandate.

This is not to say that older children and adults cannot get a broken heart or a soul wound, but the more deep-seated issues causing the fragmentation of the mind occurs in the formative years. A soul wound is created upon infliction of emotional trauma, the mind fractures to encapsulate the pain, creating a part of the core person- this is sometimes referred to as a heart part. This heart part is usually at the same age of the person when the trauma occurred. This created part of the core person holds on to the pain, so the individual can continue to function without having to deal with this pain. This is double-mindedness. There are now two distinct identities instead of one. These created heart parts have emotions, and personalities and they can manifest when triggered. With each trauma there is potential for another fracture of the mind to occur, so a person can have multiple fractures creating multiple heart parts and multiple parts of the core person. Dissociative part of the core (DPC) is not to be mistaken for a mental disorder, mental diagnosis, or alter personality. Also keep in mind the purpose of this manual is to provide a brief understanding of inner healing and why it is necessary in deliverance.

Why is inner healing important to our mental, emotional, and spiritual health?

Soul wounds, fragmentation of the mind, or dissociation of the core are used interchangeably; and can be seen as a broken heart that requires healing so the person can be made whole and be reconciled with self, neighbor, and the Lord Jesus Christ. Inner healing is very important to our mental, emotional, and spiritual health because those who have had soul wounds inflicted upon them, until they are healed will tend to live from that place of hurt. There are times the emotions are buried so deep that one is not even aware of them. However, those feelings come out when we least expect in anger, resentment, isolation, depression, and anxiety. Many times, evil spirits hide behind the inner wounds and can block deliverance. Hurt people hurt others because they connect, identify with, and behave in response to the wounds and hurt on the inside. In addition, wounded people tend to have difficulty fully connecting with God as Father and with the Holy Spirit. Often, those dealing with unhealed soul wounds are insecure in their identity. They tend to hide, isolate from certain spaces, deal with shame, and self-pity, and are usually trapped in the soul realm. Soul wounds or dissociation of the core can also lead to a root of bitterness. Hebrews 12:15 NIV tells us a bitter root causes trouble and defilement for many. Therefore, inner healing allows individuals to receive the grace of God and be restored to wholeness.

God's will for us is to be made whole so we can accomplish his purposes in the earth-Amen.

3 John 1:2 KJV reads: *Beloved, I pray that in all respects you may prosper and be in good health, just as your soul prospers.*

Inner healing is recommended to be administered alongside of deliverance.

Instructions for ministers administering deliverance:
- Do not approach deliverance in your own strength. Understand that it is the power of God working through you to set the captives free. Do not ever allow pride to set in to think it is your personal anointing that makes the demons go.

Expect to be taunted by the demons, the response should be "this is not a battle between you and me, but this battle is the Lord's."

- Ensure that all personal sins are dealt with before engaging in deliverance activity.
- Do not try to engage in deliverance if you are in active sin or if you have not overcome the vulnerable areas in your own life.
- It is recommended to work in teams, with a minimum of two people.

It is recommended to not use physical force during deliverance encounters. Ask the Holy Spirit to bind and tie up every violent spirit.

6

Phases of the Deliverance Encounter

1. **Introduction**

   - Welcome – introduce yourself and the team. Establish safe space atmosphere.

   - Brief explanation of the agenda and what to expect.

   - Opening prayer

     a. Thank the Lord for the opportunity to minister to the individual.

     b. Apply the blood of Jesus; establish your authority over the space and the encounter; ask Holy Spirit to expose all the evil he wants to deal with in this session.

     c. Bind all demonic activity; bind control, hiding and escape.

     d. Release the anointing to break every yoke.

     e. Anoint the person receiving ministry for protection against demonic assaults and violence, anoint tattoos and piercing to break every curse and ungodly soul ties connected to them.

     f. Ask Holy Spirit for angelic assistance.

     g. Draw a blood line between the deliverance minister and all demons. Demons are not permitted to touch the deliverance minister.

   Beware there may be manifestations during the prayer- do not engage in expulsion at this time. Bind every spirit that manifests; tell it to go down and be bound.

2. **Pre-ministry instructions**

   - Instruct the person to take the back seat. Do not engage, do not pray, or speak in tongues during the session. Stay in the back seat and relax. Tell them they are safe, and that God is in control of the session.

   - Instruct the person to speak what they see and hear as they hear and see it, even if it is a curse word. Allow the manifestations- do not hold back.

   - Further case investigation as needed on items identified in the Personal

Spiritual Profile (PSP) that needs clarity.

- Inform the individual the areas of evil kingdoms you identified from the PSP- by doing this, the person will know that you have taken the time to review their information, this will foster trust and comfort.

- By this time, you should have already had conversations with the individual and trust has been established.

3. Deliverance counseling

- Establish Jesus is the deliverer, their faith is to be in Jesus and not in the deliverance minister (DM).

- Explain the concept of legal rights. All legal rights must be removed to dislodge and expel the demons.

- Explain unrepented sin, active curses and dissociation of the core are what gives the demons legal rights. Explain the concept that sin is a violation of God's Word.

- Counsel on the concept and elements of forgiveness. Forgiveness is not a feeling, but a choice in obedience to God. Forgiveness opens the door for healing to begin. See Matthew 18:34-35. Forgiveness releases us.

- During the Repeat After Me phase (RAM), consisting of: RAM prayers of salvation and submission to Jesus, RAM forgiveness, RAM curse breaking and RAM self-declare, instruct that it is crucial to repeat from the heart with conviction and not just to repeat. This step is crucial to remove the legal rights the demons are holding on to and to close the doors of demonic entry.

- Explain to the individual the necessity to submit to the Lordship of Christ. Explain areas and issues that will hinder deliverance. (Lack of repentance and submission).

- Discuss the demonic re-entry clause. Matthew 12:43-45, John 5:14, Luke 11:24-26.

- Counsel the individual to decide on the boundaries needed to be put in place to keep them walking in freedom after the deliverance encounter.

- Counsel the individual that deliverance is not an intervention, but it is a process. Deuteronomy 7:22, Exodus 23:29-30. It is little by little. (More than one session maybe needed.)

- Explain the mode of demonic expulsions (DE) can be from any orifice in the human body and is not limited to vomiting. For example: yawning, coughing, the ear and nose, etc.

- Absence of manifestations or absence of vomiting doesn't mean deliverance didn't happen or will not happen, as it can happen after the person gets home.

4. Repeat After Me (RAM) Prayers

- RAM confessions of identity in Christ and declaration of their authority in Jesus. "I belong to Jesus."

- RAM confessions and repent of the sins of the ancestors. Nehemiah 1:6-7. Example: I confess the sin of witchcraft by my ancestors and my parents, and I repent of the sin of witchcraft done by my ancestors and parents, etc.

- Repent of the three pathways of sin:

    a. Personal sin- can include backsliding, prayerlessness, fornication, anger at God, etc.

    b. Sins done against those under authority- abuse from parent, pastors, etc. This is sin done against you from a person with authority over you such as in incest and rape.

    c. Sins done across the ungodly soul tie- adultery, fornication, gossip, etc.

- RAM forgiveness prayers from the heart- have the person make a mental note of those they need to forgive and have them go down their list to forgive each person, including themselves. This can be a very emotional time for the individual, give them time to process.

5. Repeat After Me (RAM)

- Curse breaking and release

    a. RAM Curse Breaking, RAM Break Soul Ties- release, forgive and bless perpetrators. Since the person has already repented of their personal sins, now they are to break the resulting curses from that sin.

    b. Example: I renounce and break every curse of premature death over my life (based on what is listed in their PSP), and in the name of Jesus I break every assignment of premature death over my life and over the lives of my children. Go through each category identified in the PSP in this manner. Example: a woman has an abortion (this act is considered murder). This sin releases a curse of death in the woman's life that could manifest in sickness, accidents, death to relationships, ministry, etc. The curse will need to be broken to stop it from its course.

c. Break ungodly soul ties- Example: "in the name of Jesus, I repent of the ungodly soul tie with _____ and I ask you to forgive me. In the name of Jesus, I hereby break this ungodly ST, I take back all they took from me, and I give back all that belongs to them." Go through breaking ST with fornication partners and every ungodly relationship.

d. Pull down ungodly strongholds in the name of Jesus. This is usually rooted in lies and false beliefs. Have the person pray truth from scripture over the strongholds.

- RAM Self-Declare for Inner Healing (IH).

- RAM- I acknowledge Holy Spirit as my helper, I speak to every part of me, every hurt part, every part that helps me, I want all parts of me to be healed. That is my will that every part of me go into arms of Jesus to be healed.

- Prophetic act of dividing soul and spirit (Hebrews 4:12).

Example: In the name of Jesus, by the authority of the Word of God (use your Bible) we divide soul and spirit and separate precious Jane from every demon spirit, and we further divide the core of Jane from every dissociated part of the core.

6. Inner Healing

- STC- Submerge the core

a. Allow the person to breathe and relax.

b. Pray Holy Spirit go to the places that need to be healed.

c. As you invite HS to go to those places, expect core and demonic interference. So, encourage the core by saying you are doing a good job, let the emotions come up, stay in the back seat, and encourage the Dissociated Parts of the Core (DPC) by saying "you are safe", and bind every demon, repeat these steps, you may lay hands to project Holy Spirit power, until the core is submerged- this will be evidenced by a subdued state as if the person is slain by the holy spirit.

d. Engage and negotiate with the parts by asking "what is your name, how old are you, what did they do to her? Expect this will take time, do not rush the process. If the DPC does not emote, then conduct a general healing by praying- every part of _____ be healed and go right into the arms of Jesus. Lay hands and repeat. Lead every part that comes up to speak or cry to the arms of Jesus to be healed.

    e. Do not attempt to give the person tissues or hug while they are in the emotional process as this will interfere and cause the DPC to go back down. Let them cry.

- If DPC does not emote or manifest, then do general healing prayers for the mind, brain, and emotions.

- Bind any demons that manifest during IH. Let the IH process run its course.

- After each DPC gets healed, invite Holy Spirit to fill the spaces vacated.

7. Deliverance Phase-after IH begin confrontation

- Confrontation of the evil spirits identified in the PSP.

- Provoke manifestations of demons- example: "In the name of Jesus GET UP AND FACE ME. Continue provocation; torment by laying on of hands or use of a blessed object can be used to provoke them, fire of God can be used to provoke them to manifestation.

- Upon manifestation, command them in the name of Jesus to tell you their name and who they report to. The goal is to identify the strongman. When the name is given, ask- "WILL THIS HOLD TRUE BEFORE THE LORD JESUS CHRIST." Command them in the name of Jesus to tell you the truth.

- When the strongman or chief spirit is identified, command them to tell you their legal right. In most cases, since we have already done IH, repentance, forgiveness and broke curses and ST- they will not have any legal rights.

- If no response, ask "do you have legal right, yes or no." Does God give you permission to stay? Yes, or no? If yes, command them to tell you what the legal right is.

- Once that legal right is identified, tell the demon to go down, bring the person up and have them repent and renounce.

- Then bring the chief demon back up to command them in the name of Jesus to remove all spiritual devices: fiery darts, rings, crowns, robes and all the sickness they caused.

- Next, in the name of Jesus, bind the chief demon to lower ranking demons and to its kingdom and command them to come out as one.

- For resistant demons, we apply the demonic expulsion protocol (DEP) to weaken the demons by telling them to repeat I _____(strongman) renounce all claims to Jane, I can't have her, I have failed in my assignment, she belongs to Jesus. I_____(strong man) bind myself to my kingdom and we all now go as one to the pit. Then command them to come out in the name of Jesus. Project Holy Spirit power by using blessed objects- lay hands, anointing oil, and Bible to drive them out. Ask for angelic assistance.

- Repeat the steps for the next kingdoms identified in the PSP. Addressing one kingdom at time. Maximum time for 1 DE is 2.5-3 hours. Remaining kingdoms after that time spent (maximum 3 hours) should be addressed at a subsequent appointment.

If something manifests that you are not sure what it is, you can ask "are you a person or a demon." There are times memories of other people will manifest in the person- those can be witches they were in contact with, could be family members, sexual partners etc., those are called soul deposits. Soul deposits are also cast out in the name of Jesus.

8. Conclusion

- HSF- Holy Spirit fill every spot vacated by evil and heart parts.

- Lay hands and release a fresh infilling of the HS.

- End of session anointing to the person.

- End of session Blessing- Mothers blessing/ Fathers blessing.

- Post ministry instructions- Email report and follow-up instructions, with emphasis on submission to God, staying connected to a Bible preaching church, staying active in prayer, discipleship, and fasting. Recommend a follow-up appointment in 2-4 weeks.

- Prepare to spend 2.5- 3 hours ministering to the individual.

Group session deliverance encounter:

- The same principles and steps apply.

- Since there will not be a PSP for the group sessions, the DM will conduct RAM confessions and curse-breaking in a general sense, calling out the most common demonic groupings and spirits.

7

Sample Repeat After Me Prayers for Deliverance

This repeat after me prayer can be used for both individual and group sessions. The person repeats after the minister.

"Dear Lord Jesus, I believe that you are the Son of God. I believe that you died on the cross for my sins, and you rose again from the grave. I believe that you are now at the right of the Father.

I accept you and confess you as my Lord and my Savior. I repent and renounce and ask for your forgiveness for every sin of rebellion and disobedience that I have committed against you.

Lord, I repent of and renounce every sinful word that I have spoken or thought about you. I break every curse brought upon me or on my family by the act of cursing God or due to blasphemy. I repent of and renounce every sinful word I have ever spoken against any of your servants. I repent for lifting my hand against your anointed ones. I repent for every sinful word I have ever spoken against my parents, and I repent for every act of dishonor I committed against my mother or my father. I break every vow and every judgement I have placed on my mother or my father for whatever they did or for whatever they did not do. In the name of Jesus, I now break every curse brought upon me by these actions.

I renounce every curse that has been passed down to me by my family or prior generations. I do not choose to participate or practice any sins of my parents or my ancestors. I forgive my parents and my ancestors for causing these curses to come upon me.

I repent of all my contacts with Satan and all his evil works. I renounce all involvement with witchcraft and the occult. I repent and renounce all demon spirits that I have allowed to enter my life. I now come out of agreement with the lies of Satan that I have believed.

Lord Jesus, I chose to forgive all those who have wronged or harmed me. I lay down all resentment, all bitterness, all hatred, and all rebellion. As an act of my free will, I forgive from my heart and release them to you: **(Call out the names of those needing to be forgiven- this may take several minutes.)**

Lord, I ask you to forgive me, I ask you to cleanse me by your precious blood. I accept your forgiveness now by faith. And I choose to forgive myself. **(Have the person reflect and forgive themselves.)**

Satan, because of the blood of Jesus, you have no power over me, and you have no place in me. I now cancel all your legal rights over me in the name of Jesus. In the name of Jesus, I declare that every demonic covenant and satanic contract working against me be annulled and destroyed by the blood of Jesus.

Lord, you have said, whosoever shall call on the name of the Lord shall be delivered. I call on your name right now to deliver me. I acknowledge you as my deliverer."

8

Sample Repeat After Me Prayer – Break Soul Ties

" Lord Jesus, I submit myself completely to you. I repent for participating or for allowing myself to get involved in any ungodly relationships with any person, place, or thing. I ask you to forgive me for all sexual misconduct and to forgive me for the ungodly soul ties with: (**name the people one by one. This should include illegal sexual partners, ungodly practice partners such as gossip, drugs, alcohol and even those co-dependent relationships**.)

And in the name of Jesus, I ask that my spirit be loosed from them. I tell my spirit to forget the unions, I tell my mind to release responsibility for them and I tell my emotions to let go and forget the union. I tell the fragmented pieces of my soul to come back together. I give back all I have of them, and I take back all they have of me in the name of Jesus. I hereby break every ungodly soul tie in the name of Jesus.

Lord, I choose to forgive each person that I have been involved with in the wrong way. I renounce all uses of my body as an instrument of unrighteousness, and I ask you to break all bondages that Satan has brought into my life through those involvements. I choose to no longer be angry, hate or punish myself and I forgive myself. I now present my body to you as a living sacrifice. I reserve the sexual use of my body only in marriage. I reject and renounce the lie of Satan that my body is not clean or is in any way unacceptable due to my past sexual experiences.

Lord, I thank you that you have totally cleansed and forgiven me and that you accept and love me unconditionally. Therefore, I accept myself and my body as clean in the name of Jesus. Amen!"

9

Sample Repeat After Me Prayer – Curse Breaking

For private session- go through each category identified on the Personal Spiritual Profile (PSP).

For the group session-Go through the most common groupings and what Holy Spirit reveals. The most common groups are Jezebel poverty, infirmity, witchcraft, mind-binding, deaf and dumb, fear, torment, heaviness, depression, death, sexual perversion, fornication, pride, mammon, and religion.

"I confess the sins of my ancestors and the sins of my parents and my personal sin of witchcraft. My parents did witchcraft, my ancestors did witchcraft, they did voodoo, they did santeria, they manipulated, they controlled. I confess and repent of the sin of witchcraft in my bloodline.

I did witchcraft, I controlled, I manipulated, I did voodoo, I repent of the sin of witchcraft, I renounce witchcraft now. I ask you, Lord, to forgive me for this sin of witchcraft. In the name of Jesus, I break the curse of witchcraft over my life, I break the power of witchcraft and its resulting curses over my life now, in the name of Jesus. I break every assignment of Satan over my life and over the lives of my children due to witchcraft. Every curse brought on me and my children due to witchcraft I renounce and break now in the name of Jesus."

Go through each category in this manner- confess the sin, the act, repent, renounce then break the curse and the assignment over the present and future generation.

EXAMPLE # 2- "In the name of Jesus I repent for coming in agreement with Jezebel. Lord, forgive me. I allowed Jezebel for too long. I repent of that sin, and I renounce Jezebel. Jezebel, in the name of Jesus, I renounce you and I break your curse right now. I release myself from you, I separate myself from you right now in the name of Jesus. Jezebel, I break your hold, your power, and your curse over me and over the lives of my children.

I renounce all your gifts in the name of Jesus. Jezebel, I resist you, take your hands off me, take your hands off my future generation, in the name of Jesus."

Repeat for each category.

When renouncing the spirit of death, include death to relationships, death to finances, death to businesses, ministry, etc.; and replace with life after breaking the curse.

10

Sample Prayer for Deliverance Minister to Pray Over the Person or Group being Ministered To

This is done before beginning the expulsion phase and after the curse breaking.

"In the name of the Lord Jesus Christ, I now bind every spirit anyway associated with _____whether in him/her, attached to him/her or anyway connected with his/her life. I now call you under the authority of the living resurrected Lord Jesus, the One who defeated your master. You are commanded that you will not harm him/her, nor leave him/her and go to someone else. I command in the name of Jesus that you will not split, divide, multiply, fragment or clone, nor use any form of demonic trickery or deception. If you have already split, divided, multiplied, fragmented, or cloned you are commanded in the name of Jesus to rejoin as one kingdom. There will be no passing on of duties nor calling on others to replace you. All traffic will be one way, and that will be out and into the abyss in the name of Jesus. I forbid use of revolving doors and entry by other demon powers. In the name of Jesus, I command that you dissolve all intentions right now. All demonic activity and works are to stop right now in the name of Jesus. All damages and disorders will be repaired and restored exactly as Jehovah God intends. Now, whether hiding or sleeping, using shelves or dark corners in the subconscious, coming, and going or floating in free circulation you are now under the authority of Jesus Christ. You are commanded in the name of Jesus that you will be obedient. All hiding places are destroyed. In the name of Jesus, I remove all crowns and robes of authority. You are commanded in the name of Jesus that you will not communicate with other demons at this time in any way to scheme, plot, plan or devise a way to retain this kingdom. In the name of Jesus, the kingdom will be demolished. In the name of Jesus, I bind every demon from lending any assistance or interference. In the name of Jesus, I command every demon to now begin to retrieve every seed that you have planted, you are commanded to uproot everything planted, nothing is to be left behind, and every doorway will be closed and locked in the name of Jesus. The command in the name of the Lord Jesus Christ is that when directed to that you go immediately into the abyss and never return. I now command in the name of the Lord Jesus Christ, that demon powers line up in order of rank, I separate the highest-ranking demon from other demon powers and command that you will stand alone gaining no strength from other evil spirits. Now, this is the command of the Lord Jesus Christ, and you must obey."

For personal session, minister will say: "What is your name, demon? In the name of the Lord Jesus Christ, you are commanded to tell me your name. I command in the name of Jesus to get up and expose yourself, what is your name? You cannot hide, in the name of Jesus you must obey, get up and expose yourself."

For group sessions, minister may say: "I command every demon in the name of Jesus to expose yourself now. Get up and expose yourself. You cannot hide, in the name of Jesus you must obey, get up and expose yourself."

Minister can apply pressure and Holy Spirit power by laying of hands or the use of a blessed object, such as a Bible. All the while commanding the demon to be exposed and say their names.

11

Post-Deliverance Instructions

1. It is important to have a follow-up appointment. The spirits will try to come back and lie to you to make you believe nothing happened at your deliverance session and you didn't really get set free. See Matthew 12:43-45, Luke 11:24-26.

2. It is important to quickly repent when falling into any kind of sin. There is no such thing as a little sin; sin is sin. You must quickly repent and ask God for forgiveness. Remember, sin gives legal rights to demon spirits. See *Ephesians 4:27, and do not give the devil a foothold.*

3. Many behaviors come from habits we developed and lies we believed, and it will take time to develop a new and healthy belief system that will help to produce new healthy behaviors and habits.

4. Meditate on the word of God daily, challenge your thoughts, replace lies with truth found in God's word, and speak affirmations from the word of God over your life.

5. It is crucial to remain connected in a spiritual community, such as a church and be accountable to your spiritual leader. Share your deliverance experience with your Pastor and give them permission to hold you accountable.

12

Recommendations to Walking Out Your Freedom

1. Submit every area of your life to the Lordship of Christ. Resist the devil, be quick to repent of sin, be quick to forgive others. Live a life of prayer and devotion to God. John 1:11-12, James 4:7, Matthew 7, 1 John 1:9.

2. Continually be filled with the Holy Spirit. Ephesians 5:18, Romans 8:13, Galatians 5:16-26

3. Live by the Word of God. Luke 11:13, Matthew 4:4-11, Ephesians 6:10-18.

4. Renew your mind daily with Bible reading and meditation. Romans 12:1-2. 2 Corinthians 10:3-5, Colossians 3:1-2.

5. Strengthen your spirit man by reading and confessing God's word consistently. Mark 11:22-25, Ephesians 1:3-23, Ephesians 3:16-20, 2 Timothy 3:16-17.

6. Practice praise and worship always. Isaiah 61:3, Isaiah 60:18, Hebrews 13:15

7. Cultivate healthy relationships. Matthew 18:15-20, 1 John 1:7, 1 John 2:9-11.

8. Sever unhealthy relationships and avoid those situations and relations that can negatively influence you. James 4:4, 1 Corinthians 15:33

9. Connect with a healthy Holy Spirit-filled, Bible-preaching church community.

10. Share the gospel message with others and proclaim the word of God. Hebrews 3:1, 4:14, 10:23.

11. Do not harbor unforgiveness; do not live with offense in your heart and be quick to forgive others when they sin against you. Matthew 18

12. Remain humble. James 4:6.

13. Use your authority in Jesus Christ. Enforce your identity in Christ. Matthew 16:19, 1 Peter 2:9

Deliverance needs to be "**walked out.**" Make a commitment to yourself to walk out your deliverance and maintain your freedom.

13

Preparing for Deliverance

Questions and Answers

Is your problem demonic?

• All problems are not demonic! We do have a free will. We cannot blame demons for everything.

• You may need deliverance if there is a driving force behind your problem.

• You may need deliverance if you still have oppression after you have applied the Word, spiritual discipline, and prayed for relief.

• You may need deliverance if you have an infirmity and doctors cannot find it or the cause.

• You can be assured that the demonic kingdom has a plan for your life, and that is to steal, kill, and destroy. You can be confident that demonic entities have been assigned to you. If you have oppressions that characterize these descriptions, where you cannot get or maintain victory in your life, you may need deliverance.

How can I prepare for my deliverance?

• You must really want it. Stir up your faith. Your participation is necessary.

• Circle all items on the Demonic Strongholds list, past or present that may apply.

• <u>Put significant time, effort, and prayer into working on the "Demonic Strongholds Entry Points List."</u> This is key! The effectiveness of your deliverance is directly related to this. Do not leave it to the last minute!

• Do a house cleaning in the natural. Get rid of all pagan idols, items that spirits can be attached to, and pornographic materials in your household.

• Pray, and if possible, fast before your deliverance.

How can I assist during my deliverance?

• Arrive on time for your deliverance prayer. Wear comfortable clothes. Do not let anything interfere with this day in your life!

• Be completely honest about listing the strongholds in your life in your homework.

Details are not necessary (God already knows, and those who pray for you are trained and trustworthy). The demonic kingdom needs to see that you are serious about this!

- Do not pray, worship, talk or pray in tongues during the session. Words can create a blockage. Only agree, in your mind, for the spirits to leave. Agree in your mind with what the minister is praying. Do not hold back your emotions or reactions. Many evil spirits are expelled by the mouth. Don't be embarrassed to cough, burp, yawn, sigh, scream, or spit up. It's only an evil spirit on its way out. However, there may be no physical reaction at all.

What can hinder my deliverance?

- Not doing the homework...preparing the entry points list and then making the declarations boldly, out loud and in faith!
- Unconfessed sin or ongoing sin that you are trying to hide. You must want your freedom for you!
- Bottom line: if you do not prepare, do not do the homework, and do not want to be free, then it is very unlikely that you will be delivered!

Summary of Instructions

- Make declarations out loud the night/day before the deliverance session.
- Bring the "Entry Points" List with you to the session.
- Bring the "Strongholds/Issues" List, word curses and known generational curses to the session.

14

Personal Consent to Receive Ministry

I do hereby affirm and state that I, _____ consent for _____ to minister to me in the areas of Spiritual Counseling, Personal Ministry and the Ministry of Deliverance.

I understand and acknowledge that all ministers either Licensed or Lay that are involved in this ministry are not licensed or trained as psychotherapists, mental health professionals or professional counselors.

All guidance, counsel, and advice that I receive will be solely based on Scriptural principles and Christian biblical standards as spelled out in the Holy Bible, the written Word of God.

I further understand and acknowledge that all ministry is under the direction and control of the Holy Spirit, and that no guarantees are made, nor can be made, with regard to my healing and/or deliverance.

I state that I have voluntarily sought this ministry for myself and that I hereby release the ministers and all volunteers working with_____,from any and all claims of actual or implied liability that may arise now or in the future as a result of the ministry I receive.

Signed: _____ **Date:** _____

Witnessed: _____ **Date:** _____

15

Demonic Strongholds Entry Points

- **GENERATIONAL/WORD CURSES:** List any known generational curses and word curses spoken over your life. Name the person who spoke this. (Write on back of "Strongholds List"; not on this page!)

- **UNFORGIVENESS:** List all the people from childhood to the present whom you now have or have ever had any unforgiveness or resentment towards (even if they are dead, and even you have already forgiven).

- **OCCULT:** List all dealings you have had with the occult (example: ouija, seances, hypnosis, horoscope, new age, superstition, witchcraft, oaths, santeria, palm reader, roots, martial arts, new age healing, etc.

- **SEXUAL SIN:** List all people you have been sexually involved with outside of marriage (example: rape, molestation, incest, homosexuality/lesbian, bestiality, even your spouse if you came together sexually before marriage).

- **SOUL TIES:** List all people (dead or alive) that have had an ungodly control over you. Also list your: mother, father, step-parents, spouse(s), grandparents, boss, spirit guides, abortions, hypnotist, brothers/sisters (step or half), children (step, adopted, foster), etc.

- **COVENANT, VOWS:** List all broken covenants and vows of the past (marriages, church memberships, foreclosures, private vows to God or other people, etc.)

- **PRIDE:** List everything you are prideful of. (example: do you feel you have a better marriage than others, a better ministry, a better profession, know more Bible than others).

- **IDOLATRY:** List all areas of idolatry. What stands (or has stood between you and God (example: spouse, home, job/position, money, children, etc.)

- **UNCONFESSED SIN:** List "hidden sin" or anything you've not confessed or repented of before God.

16

What Forgiveness Is

1. Forgiveness is a command.
    a. One of the biggest mistakes we could ever make is thinking forgiveness is an option. It is not an option, it is a commandment
    b. Unforgiveness is a sin issue
2. Forgiveness is releasing them to God, it is turning them over to God.

Matthew 6:14-15 says, *For if you forgive men their trespasses, your heavenly Father will also forgive you. But if you do not forgive their trespasses, neither will your Father forgive your trespasses.*

We have to understand we have absolutely no right to hold anyone in unforgiveness. God will not tolerate us doing so and "anyone" includes you. You must forgive yourself.

"Anyone" also includes God. If you blame God or you are mad at Him, you need to forgive Him.

How To Forgive
1. Get alone and ask the Lord to show you the people you need to forgive.
2. Write down names of people you need to forgive, by making a list. (They may be the little girl from the third grade, my fifth grade school teacher, etc.)
3. Be sure you include yourself.
4. Be sure to include God.
5. Go over each name with the Lord and express to Him how they have hurt you.
6. Write down what they did and why you need to forgive them. (Example: Mrs. Smith, my fifth-grade teacher, humiliated me. She made fun of me and I was so angry. I was so vulnerable and not able to protect myself from her).

7. List whatever feelings you had and the degree to which you felt them. (Example: I was so angry, I did not care if they fell and hurt themselves, actually I wish they had, etc. I wished I could have died because of the humiliation).

8. Then choose to forgive and release them. Then do it. Say something like, "Lord I choose to forgive and release ____" (name the person).

9. Write a letter to each person. "I forgive and release you from _____. "

10. Not all letters will be sent. These are an act of faith. The Lord will see you are serious.

11. Last of all, this step can be the hardest but also the most freeing. Get some tissues and go somewhere alone, the bathroom, or your bedroom with a mirror. Look at yourself in the mirror. Forgive and release yourself for everything that you need to forgive yourself of. Have lots of tissue.

Conclusion

Forgiveness will release us from the tormentors! It will also allow God to make us the man or woman of God He has called us to be.

Bibliography

Boehm, Roger. 2006. *In the face of Evil, A Wakeup Call for Christians*. Dallas, GA: Zondervan Publishing.

Chase, Mark. 2020. *The Children's Bread, And The Debate of Whether A Christian Can Have A Demon*. USA: Parables Publishing.

Duncan-Williams, Nicholas. 2012. *Binding The Strong Man*. Columbia, MD: Published by Duncan-Williams, Nicholas.

Hammond, Frank & Ida Mae. 2011. *Pigs In The Parlor, Study Guide*. USA: Impact Christian Books.

Larson, Bob. 2013. *Curse Breaking, Freedom From The Bondage of Generational Sin*. Shippensburg, PA: Destiny Image Publishing.

Larson, Bob. 2016. *Dealing with Demons, An Introductory Guide to Exorcism and Discerning Evil Spirits*. Shippensburg, PA: Destiny Image Publishing.

Maldonado, Guillermo. 2007. *Inner Healing and Deliverance*. Miami, FL: ERJ Publications.

Pagani, Alexander. 2018. *The Secrets To Deliverance, Defeat the Toughest Cases of Demonic Bondage*. Lake Mary, FL: Charisma House Publishing.

Sudduth, William. 2013. *Deliverance Training Manual*. Colorado Springs, CO: RAM, Inc. Publishing.

Graphics and Images: Courtesy of Invicta University School of Deliverance Ministry and Inner Healing. www.invicta.university.com

Forms: Courtesy of Piper, Lisa. Driven to be Free Ministry. www.driventobefree.org.

Confidential Information/Personal Spiritual Profile:

This form is to be completed and returned at least 7 days before

the private session deliverance encounter.

OPEN DOORS & IDENTIFICATION OF STRONGHOLDS

Generational Issues (list i.e.: addition, divorce, perversion, poverty, etc.) _____

_____

_____

_____

SPIRIT of FEAR
- ☐ Insecurity
- ☐ Inadequacy
- ☐ Inferiority
- ☐ Timidity
- ☐ Rejection
- ☐ Feel not good enough
- ☐ Worry/Anxiety
- ☐ Sensitivity to Words/Actions
- ☐ Cowardice
- ☐ Hiding/Escaping
- ☐ Fear of Authority
- ☐ Fear of being Abandoned
- ☐ Victimization
- ☐ Migraines
- ☐ Panic Attacks
- ☐ Nervousness
- ☐ Dread
- ☐ Procrastinate
- ☐ Phobias: Click or tap here to enter text.
- ☐ Feeling of Fear in your room or home
- ☐ Night Terrors/Bad Dreams

Spirit of Slumber
- ☐ Isolation/Anti-Social
- ☐ Sleepiness/Laziness
- ☐ Forgetfulness
- ☐ Stupidity
- ☐ Daydreaming/Trances
- ☐ Apathy/Indifference
- ☐ Confusion

SPIRIT of PRIDE
- ☐ Pride/Vanity
- ☐ Overbearing/Domineering
- ☐ Rebellion
- ☐ Always right
- ☐ Impatient
- ☐ Perfection
- ☐ Accusation/Scorn
- ☐ Judgmental/condemning
- ☐ Self-Judgment/Self-Condemning
- ☐ Competition
- ☐ Mockery
- ☐ Stubbornness
- ☐ Self-righteousness
- ☐ Mockery
- ☐ Stubbornness
- ☐ Self-Righteousness
- ☐ Embarrassment/Humiliation
- ☐ False Humility
- ☐ Bragging & Boastful
- ☐ Arrogant
- ☐ Gossip
- ☐ Boastful
- ☐ Sarcasm
- ☐ Critical & Fault Finding
- ☐ Muscle Cramps
- ☐ Sleepiness when near anointing

Whoredoms
- ☐ Worldliness
- ☐ Idolatry
- ☐ Fornication and/or Adultery
- ☐ Love of Money
- ☐ Harlotry
- ☐ Love of: control, power, money, materialism, self
- ☐ Pornography
- ☐ Baal/Bel Worship
- ☐ All unfaithfulness
- ☐ Excessive Appetites
- ☐ Hoarding

SPIRIT of Heaviness
- ☐ Depression
- ☐ Gloomy/Sadness
- ☐ Rejection, ☐ Self-Rejection
- ☐ Fear of Rejection
- ☐ Hopelessness
- ☐ False Responsibly
- ☐ Results of Sexual Abuse
- ☐ Inferiority/Low Self- Esteem
- ☐ Excessive Mourning
- ☐ Grief – Broken Heart
- ☐ Fatigue ☐ Self-Pity
- ☐ Guilty/Shame
- ☐ Insomnia ☐ Loneliness
- ☐ Suppressed Emotions (fear, anger, rage, violence, hatred)
- ☐ Self-Hate
- ☐ Gluttony, Bulimia, Anorexia, Binging
- ☐ Feeling of Gloom over you
- ☐ Arms and legs often feel heavy
- ☐ Foggy mind
- ☐ Difficulty making decisions because it feels overwhelming

Lying Spirit
- ☐ Exaggeration/Drama
- ☐ Gossip
- ☐ Strong deception
- ☐ Slander - Accusations
- ☐ Self-Deception
- ☐ Flattery
- ☐ False Prophesies
- ☐ Hypocrisy
- ☐ Word Twisting
- ☐ Guilt – shame & condemnation
- ☐ False Burdens ☐ Profanity
- ☐ Stealing & Cheating
- ☐ Superstition & old wives' tales
- ☐ Religious/legalism/Tradition
- ☐ Homosexuality
- ☐ Gender Confusion
- ☐ Frenzied emotional actions
- ☐ Breaking Covenants

Page 1 www.respiteforchange.com Modified and Added to from lists used from other ministries & Deliverance Training Manual by Dr. William Sudduth

48

Anti-Christ Spirit
☐ Doubt & Unbelief
☐ Rebellion
☐ Humanism/Intellectualism
☐ Self-Exaltation
☐ New Age
☐ Jezebel and/or Ahab
☐ Worldy Speech and actions
☐ Profanity
☐ Denies Deity, atonement or Christ's Teachings
☐ Unable to listen during preaching
☐ Mocking in head when minister is preaching or during times of anointing
☐ Kundalini Yoga
☐ Anger or hatred of God
☐ Lawlessness and Rebellion
☐ False Religions
☐ Idolatry
☐ Legalism, ritualism, formalism
☐ Rock Music, Rap Music, Hip Hop, New Age Music or any ungodly music
☐ Secret Societies
☐ Serpent Spirits
☐ Accusing
☐ Deceiver

Bondage
☐ Hindering
☐ Greed/Hoarding
☐ Gluttony
☐ Slavery to Sin
☐ Emotional Weakness
☐ Any Addictions
☐ Mind Binding Spirit
☐ Religions/Legalism Bondage
☐ Traditions of Men
☐ Insecurity or Fear
☐ Injustice
☐ Idolatry
☐ Lust and Perversion
☐ Compulsive Behavior

Deaf & Dumb Spirit
☐ Double Mindedness
☐ Can't Understand
☐ Suicide/Self- Mutilation
☐ Mind Binding
☐ Seizures/Epilepsy
☐ Mental Illness & Insanity
☐ Dumb and/or deaf
☐ Retardation
☐ Palsy
☐ Hallucinations
☐ Self-Harm/Punishment
☐ ADD – ADHD – LD
☐ Disassociate Disorder
☐ Crippling
☐ Burning
☐ Ear Problems
☐ Crying/Tearing
☐ Alzheimer's
☐ Prostration
☐ Eating Disorders
☐ Gnashing of teeth
☐ Self-Hatred
☐ Zombie Spirit (numb/dumb)

Poverty
☐ Poverty Mentality
☐ Lack
☐ Things Break Abnormally
☐ Hoarding
☐ Cannot be satisfied
☐ Do not Tithe
☐ Difficulty Giving
☐ Difficult time using what you have for fear you won't have more in the future

Jealousy Spirit
☐ Selfish
☐ Bitterness/Negativity
☐ Blaming
☐ Envy/Covetousness
☐ Control/Jezebel/Manipulation
☐ Revenge & Retaliation
☐ Suspicion
☐ Hatred/Self-Hatred
☐ Murder & Violence
☐ Profanity
☐ Anger/Rage
☐ Strife/Division/Conflict
☐ Bigotry & Racism
☐ Vigilante Spirit
☐ Passive Aggressive
☐ Extreme Competition
☐ Can't reason & Argumentative
☐ Cruelty - Abuse & Abuser
☐ Can do things better in mind than others doing it
☐ Cannot be happy when good things happen to others

Familiar Spirits
☐ Fear ☐ Pride ☐ Deaf & Dumb
☐ Slumber ☐ Heaviness
☐ Jealousy ☐ Lying
☐ Anti-Christ ☐ Poverty & Lack
☐ Bondage & Addictions
☐ Infirmity ☐ Whoredoms
☐ Perversion ☐ Word Curses
☐ Divination/Occult/Witchcraft
☐ Spirit Guides ☐ Freemasonry
☐ Slavery ☐ Bigotry & Racism
☐ Visited by or see dead people in dreams or in person

Perversion

- [ ] Lust
- [ ] Twisting the Word
- [ ] Doctrinal Error
- [ ] Satanic Ritual Abuse
- [ ] Rape, Sodomy
- [ ] Chronic Worrier
- [ ] Egocentric Thinking
- [ ] S&M
- [ ] Effeminate (male)
- [ ] Masculine (female)
- [ ] Contentious and foolish
- [ ] Prostitution
- [ ] Exposure and voyeurism
- [ ] Atheist
- [ ] Filthy mind
- [ ] Orgies
- [ ] Satanic dedications and marriage ceremonies
- [ ] A Broken Spirit
- [ ] Uncleanness & Lewdness
- [ ] Illegitimacy
- [ ] Sexual Perversions
- [ ] Incest
- [ ] Pornography
- [ ] Masturbation
- [ ] Prostitution
- [ ] Self-Lover - Narcissist
- [ ] Child Molestation
- [ ] Seducing Spirit
- [ ] Fantasy Spirit
- [ ] Sensual Thoughts
- [ ] Lying
- [ ] Abortion
- [ ] Gender Confusion
- [ ] Fornication and Adultery
- [ ] All sexual demons (incubus, succubus, lilith)
- [ ] Your eyes wander to look sexually at other people and you do not want them to do so.
- [ ] Dreams: of perversion, having sex with people not your spouse, experiencing molestation by an entity

Infirmity

- [ ] Family Illness
- [ ] Death
- [ ] Arthritis/Hay Fever/Allergies/Asthma
- [ ] Heart Disease
- [ ] Cancer
- [ ] Parkinson's Disease
- [ ] Circulatory/HBP
- [ ] Disorders
- [ ] Syndromes
- [ ] Bent Spine & body
- [ ] Neck & back problems
- [ ] Bi-Polar
- [ ] Impotent
- [ ] All mental illness
- [ ] Hormone imbalance
- [ ] Chemical imbalance
- [ ] Diabetes
- [ ] All oppression
- [ ] Pain and affliction
- [ ] All lingering disorders
- [ ] Migraines
- [ ] TB & emphysema
- [ ] Blood disorder
- [ ] Fibromyalgia
- [ ] Female problems
- [ ] Alzheimer and Dementia
- [ ] Scoliosis
- [ ] All depression
- [ ] Tumors, cysts, and growths
- [ ] Weakness – tiredness & fatigue
- [ ] All infections (viral, bacterial, strep & staph)
- [ ] STDs
- [ ] Epilepsy and Seizures
- [ ] Fear of infirmity, sickness and disease
- [ ] Hypochondria

Death

- [ ] Accidents
- [ ] Assault
- [ ] Injury
- [ ] Illness
- [ ] Infirmity
- [ ] Random acts of Violence
- [ ] Disease
- [ ] Cancer
- [ ] Suicide
- [ ] Murder
- [ ] Fighting
- [ ] Clumsiness
- [ ] HIV/AIDS
- [ ] Hep C
- [ ] Abortion
- [ ] Miscarriages
- [ ] Destruction
- [ ] Dreams of death, murder, or seeing grim reaper

Seducing Spirit

- [ ] Seared Conscience
- [ ] All deception
- [ ] Vigilante Spirit
- [ ] Fascination to
  - [ ] evil ways
  - [ ] evil objects
  - [ ] evil person
  - [ ] evil images
- [ ] Seducing and enticing
- [ ] Flirtation
- [ ] Double Standard
- [ ] Jezebel – Ahab
- [ ] Attraction to and fascination to:
  - [ ] False Prophet
  - [ ] False signs and wonders
  - [ ] Demonic movies, videos, games
  - [ ] Sexual movies, videos, games
  - [ ] Internet pornography

Divination - Witchcraft

- ☐ Lust for power and control
- ☐ Fortune teller, soothsayer, psychics
- ☐ Water spirits (pride, sexual, etc.)
- ☐ Stargazer, zodiac, horoscopes
- ☐ False Prophets
- ☐ Warlock, witch, sorcerer, wizard
- ☐ Mind-control
- ☐ Manipulation and control
- ☐ Automatic hand-writing and hand-writing analysis
- ☐ Shaman and witchdoctor
- ☐ All spirit guides
- ☐ All animal guides
- ☐ All Indian witchcraft
- ☐ Astral-projection
- ☐ Druid and Celtic witchcraft
- ☐ Occultism and syncretism
- ☐ Rebellion
- ☐ Hypnotism, enchanting
- ☐ Acupuncture
- ☐ Drug use, illegal or prescription
- ☐ Birth charts
- ☐ All magic, black or white
- ☐ A serpent spirit
- ☐ Vampire fascination
- ☐ Mermaid fascination
- ☐ Spiritism
- ☐ Jezebel
- ☐ Water witching and divination
- ☐ WICCA
- ☐ Numerology and reflexology
- ☐ Harry Potter
- ☐ Voodoo and Santeria
- ☐ Imaginary friends
- ☐ Island witchcraft
- ☐ Gypsy
- ☐ Satanism
- ☐ Superstitions and old wife's tales
- ☐ Charms
- ☐ Fascination with evil
- ☐ Charismatic witchcraft

Divination – Witchcraft continued

- ☐ Necromancy (talking to dead)
- ☐ Yoga and all mantras
- ☐ Chants and spells
- ☐ Clairvoyance
- ☐ Spells, Hexes, Voodoo, Curses, Incantations
- ☐ Freemasonry
- ☐ Tattoos & piercings
- ☐ Satanic contracts and agreements
- ☐ Demonic movies, games, books and music
- ☐ There is someone in your life who manipulates you.
- ☐ You manipulate others
- ☐ There is someone I your life who seeks to control you.
- ☐ You try to control others.
- ☐ Dreams of people in dark hoods, rituals, chanting

Error

- ☐ Hypocrisy
- ☐ False Doctrines - Teaching
- ☐ Twisting Scripture
- ☐ Unteachable Spirit
- ☐ Mixing holy with profane
- ☐ Defensive and argumentative
- ☐ Sympathy for the devil
- ☐ Having a form of godliness but denying its power
- ☐ Mental confusion and fear
- ☐ Dullness of comprehension
- ☐ Hyper-spiritual
- ☐ Gender/Sexual Confusion

Page 4 www.respiteforchange.com. Modified and Added to from lists used from other ministries & Deliverance Training Manual by Dr. William Sudduth

51

Trauma – Inner Healing Issues

☐ Accidents
☐ Rape, Molestation
☐ Subjected to Pornography
☐ Witness abuse
☐ Experienced abuse
☐ Grew up in home of addiction
☐ Abandoned by a parent(s)
☐ Adoption
☐ Abortion
☐ Divorce (self)
☐ Divorce (parents)
☐ Subjected to child going through trauma
☐ Illness
☐ Church hurt
☐ Bullied
☐ Mistreated
☐ Grew up in poverty
☐ Neglected
☐ In Foster Care System
☐ Parent(s) wanted a different gender
☐ Parent(s) said they wish you weren't born
☐ Parent(s) spoke word curses over you
☐ Trauma from school
☐ Trauma from witnessing other family issues
☐ Dreams of being a child or feeling like a child/child-lie tendencies

QUESTIONS:

What would you like God to deliver you from?
Click or tap here to enter text.

The keys to deliverance are the following: (Check the area the best describes you:

Key	I have.	I will.	I won't.	I don't know how
Repent	☐	☐	☐	☐
Forgive	☐	☐	☐	☐
Cut Soul Ties	☐	☐	☐	☐
Renounce Family Sin	☐	☐	☐	☐
Cut off Word Curses	☐	☐	☐	☐
Renounce Lies	☐	☐	☐	☐
Stop Sinning	☐	☐	☐	☐
Remove ungodliness from home/car/person	☐	☐	☐	☐
Confessed Jesus as your Savior	☐	☐	☐	☐

1. Do you have any vivid memories that torment you? ☐ Yes ☐ No
2. List any nicknames you had growing up: Click or tap here to enter text.
3. What age were you in the first memory that you have of your life? Click or tap here to enter text.
4. If you have done someone wrong, would you be willing to apologize and/or make restitution? Click or tap here to enter text.
5. Do you have manifestations of an unclean spirit in your body? ☐ Yes ☐ No   If yes, what has happened to you? Click or tap here to enter text.
6. Is there anything else you would want someone praying for you to know: Click or tap here to enter text.

Page 5 www.respiteforchange.com. Modified and Added to from lists used from other ministries & Deliverance Training Manual by Dr. William Sudduth

52

My Notes

_____

_____

_____

_____

_____

_____

_____

_____

_____

_____

_____

_____

_____

_____

_____

_____

My Notes

_____

_____

_____

_____

_____

_____

_____

_____

_____

_____

_____

_____

_____

_____

My Notes

_____

_____

_____

_____

_____

_____

_____

_____

_____

_____

_____

_____

_____

_____

Deliverance Ministry Made Simple

My Notes

_____

_____

_____

_____

_____

_____

_____

_____

_____

_____

_____

_____

_____

My Notes

www.ingramcontent.com/pod-product-compliance
Lightning Source LLC
Chambersburg PA
CBHW081725120626
46550CB00010B/3248